Let Freedom Ring

Anne Hutchinson
Religious Reformer

by Mélina Mangal

Consultant:
Betty Mitchell
Professor of History
University of Massachusetts Dartmouth
North Dartmouth, Massachusetts

Capstone
press
Mankato, Minnesota

Capstone Press
151 Good Counsel Drive • P.O. Box 669 • Mankato, Minnesota 56002
http://www.capstonepress.com

Library of Congress Cataloging-in-Publication Data
Mangal, Mélina.
Anne Hutchinson: religious reformer / by Mélina Mangal.
p. cm.—(Let freedom ring)
Summary: A biography of the Puritan woman who was banished from the
Massachusetts Bay Colony for disagreeing with the prevailing religious practices.
Includes bibliographical references and index.
ISBN 0-7368-2454-5 (hardcover)
1. Hutchinson, Anne—Juvenile literature. 2. Puritans—Massachusetts—Biography—
Juvenile literature. 3. Massachusetts—History—Colonial period, ca. 1600–1775—Juvenile
literature. [1. Hutchinson, Anne. 2. Puritans. 3. Massachusetts—History—Colonial period,
ca. 1600–1775. 4. Freedom of religion—History. 5. Women—Biography.] I. Title. II. Series.
F67.H92M36 2004
974.4'02'092—dc21
                                                                2003011353

Editorial Credits
Donald Lemke, editor; Kia Adams, series designer; Enoch Peterson, book designer;
    Jo Miller, photo researcher; Eric Kudalis, product planning editor

Photo Credits
Art Resource/Tate Gallery Painting by George Morland, 9
Bridgeman Art Library/Private Collection, 11
Corbis/Bettmann, cover, 10, 13, 15, 29, 32, 34, 37; Kevin Fleming, 41
Corel/painting by George H. Boughton, 25
Getty Images Inc./Hulton/Archive, 6, 40
North Wind Picture Archives, 5, 18, 21, 26, 30, 31, 38, 42, 43

1   2   3   4   5   6   09   08   07   06   05   04

Table of Contents

Features

Chapter One

Hutchinson on Trial

Anne Hutchinson stood in the cold meetinghouse on a November morning in 1637. The room was crowded with 49 General Court members. They were all men. Hutchinson was 46 years old and pregnant for the 16th time. She did not have a lawyer, but she was ready for trial.

Governor John Winthrop of the Massachusetts Bay Colony stared at her from behind a table. "Mrs. Hutchinson," he said, "you are called here as one of those that have troubled the peace of the commonwealth and the churches here."

Hutchinson had been holding meetings to discuss religion. The court members believed this practice was wrong. They thought only male ministers could explain the word of God.

In November 1637, Hutchinson went on trial in the Massachusetts Bay Colony for holding religious meetings in her home.

Women were not supposed to express opinions about religion. The court expected her to apologize and promise to stop the meetings.

Hutchinson refused to apologize. She did not believe it was wrong to express her beliefs. "What law have I broken?" she asked.

Governor John Winthrop of the Massachusetts Bay Colony believed Hutchinson's ideas were dangerous. He forced her to leave the area forever.

Winthrop said that she had dishonored the ministers of the church by continuing to hold meetings. The court believed that these were serious crimes.

Hutchinson remained confident. She defended herself by using quotes from the Bible. As the day came to an end, it appeared as if Hutchinson was winning the case.

The next morning, Hutchinson continued to argue with the court members. She explained how God had told her about the trial. She also said that God would curse the court for punishing her.

Winthrop and the other court members were stunned. They did not believe it was possible for an ordinary person to communicate with God. Most of them thought Hutchinson was lying.

"Mrs. Hutchinson . . . is unfit for our society," said Governor Winthrop. "She shall be **banished** out of our liberties and imprisoned till she be sent away." The other members of the court agreed. Hutchinson was forced to leave the Massachusetts Bay Colony forever.

Chapter Two

Early Life and Religion

In July 1591, Anne Hutchinson was born in Alford, a town in Lincolnshire, England. She was the second of 13 children. Her mother, Bridget Dryden, was from a **Puritan** family. Anne's father, Francis Marbury, had been a minister at St. Wilfrid's church in Alford.

The year before Anne was born, Francis Marbury was banned from St. Wilfrid's. He was not allowed to preach because he had criticized, or complained about, church leaders.

Instead of working as a minister, Francis became a farmer. He also taught Anne about religion. Anne's younger brothers attended school. Girls were not allowed to go to school at that time. Anne learned at home from the Bible and her father's writings. She grew up with strong religious beliefs.

Anne grew up in a small country town similar to the one in this painting by George Morland (1763-1804).

The Church of England

In the 1500s, most people in England were Catholic. The leader of the Catholic Church was the pope. In 1509, Henry VIII, shown below, became king of England. Several years later, he wanted to change some of the church rules about divorce. The pope did not agree. King Henry decided to break away from the Catholic Church and create the Church of England. The king or queen ruled this church. They made laws about how people should worship.

In the late 1500s, a group of people became unhappy with the Church of England. They wanted to get rid of some of the church's traditions. These people, who became known as Puritans, wanted a simpler form of religion. They thought church practices should come directly from the Bible.

The Big City

In 1605, Anne's father became head of a church in London. He decided to move the family to the city. This was a big move for Anne. She was only 14 years old and grew up in a small country town. At least 225,000 people lived in London.

During the early 1600s, many people moved to London from the English countryside. The city quickly became a center for entertainment and trade.

The city was full of theaters, markets, and streets crowded with people. But Anne's life revolved around her family and church.

The Marbury family worked hard. Anne's father worked in two churches at the same time. Anne was the oldest daughter at home. She helped take care of her younger brothers and sisters. Anne also helped her mother during the birth of three babies. She learned to care for the sick at church. She also learned how to make healing **remedies** and treat wounds.

Soon, everything in Anne's life changed. In 1611, her father died. Anne and her family had to move to another house. About a year later, William Hutchinson came to visit. He was a cloth seller and sheep farmer from Alford. On August 9, 1612, Anne married William. She was 21 years old.

During the 1600s, family members or friends often helped
women during childbirth. Anne helped her mother during the
birth of three babies.

Chapter Three

A New Religion

Anne and William Hutchinson moved back to Alford and started a family. In 1613, the first of their 15 children was born. His name was Edward. The couple prayed for their new child to stay healthy.

Anne Hutchinson wanted a religious leader to guide her faith. She heard about a Puritan minister named John Cotton. Hutchinson and her husband traveled by horse and buggy 24 miles (39 kilometers) to hear him preach. The trip took almost a day each way, but the Hutchinsons visited Cotton's church many times.

The minister's sermons excited and inspired Hutchinson. She became his student. Hutchinson and Cotton also became good friends. Soon, Hutchinson began holding meetings for women in her home to share Cotton's ideas.

The teachings of Puritan minister John Cotton (1584–1652) inspired
Hutchinson to begin holding religious meetings in her home.

John Cotton preached about the Covenant of Grace. The Covenant of Grace taught that all people could go to heaven if they had faith in God. The Church of England preached a Covenant of Works. The Covenant of Works taught that in order to get to heaven, people must obey the rules from the Bible. Church leaders enforced these rules.

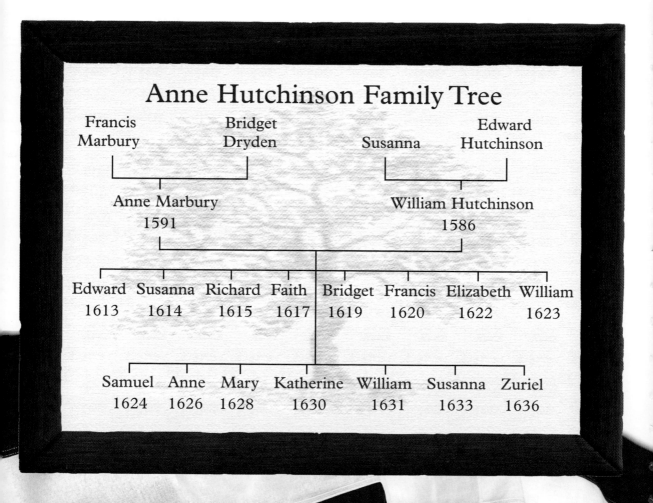

Anne Hutchinson Family Tree

Francis Marbury — Bridget Dryden

Susanna — Edward Hutchinson

Anne Marbury 1591

William Hutchinson 1586

Edward	Susanna	Richard	Faith	Bridget	Francis	Elizabeth	William
1613	1614	1615	1617	1619	1620	1622	1623

Samuel	Anne	Mary	Katherine	William	Susanna	Zuriel
1624	1626	1628	1630	1631	1633	1636

Large Families

During the 1600s, harsh living conditions, diseases, and accidents took the lives of many children. Hutchinson's brother Anthony died as a baby. Her brothers John and Daniel also died young. Later, Hutchinson's son William and two of her daughters died.

In the 1600s, women had many babies. Women got married and began having children around the ages of 14 and 15. They often had 12 to 18 babies. Hutchinson's parents had 13 children together. Hutchinson and William had 15 children.

Questioning the Rules

In 1625, Charles I became King of England. He threatened to punish anyone who did not follow the Church of England. The king's men arrested John Cotton. Church of England authorities did not approve of the way he preached.

Hutchinson began to question the rules of the Church of England. One rule required church members to climb a set of stairs to take **communion**.

Climbing the stairs was difficult for pregnant women. Authorities in the church would not change the rule. The rule seemed harsh to Hutchinson. Because she and William disagreed with the church, they began to fear for their future. They worried that the king's men might punish them next.

In 1630, many people left England to escape the plague. The skeletons in this painting represent the deadly disease.

The Plague

In 1630, the bubonic plague spread through many parts of England and the world. This disease was so serious that some people called it the Black Death. People who caught the disease became terribly ill and often died. The plague spread quickly because many people lived in cramped, dirty conditions. Rats carried the disease. Fleas would bite the rats and then bite people, spreading the disease. Thousands of people died throughout Asia and Europe.

The Hutchinsons also worried about getting sick. In 1630, a deadly disease called the **plague** spread through Alford. Many people died, including two of Hutchinson's daughters.

In 1633, John Cotton moved to the Massachusetts Bay Colony to avoid being sent to prison. With her minister gone, Hutchinson struggled with the death of her children. She also found it difficult to deal with church laws. Eventually, Hutchinson and her family decided to sail to the New World.

Chapter Four

The Massachusetts Bay Colony

In July 1634, Hutchinson and her family set sail aboard the *Griffin*. The long trip across the ocean was very uncomfortable. To pass the time, Hutchinson directed women's meetings. She also criticized the sermons of the ship's preacher, the Reverend Zechariah Symmes. He threatened to report her to church leaders when they arrived in the Massachusetts Bay Colony.

Hutchinson caused more trouble when she described her **revelations**, or visions, from God. Puritans did not believe it was possible for ordinary people to have revelations. To prove she was having these visions, Hutchinson told everyone the exact date the *Griffin* would reach Boston. The ship arrived on September 18, 1634, just as she predicted. Immediately after landing, Reverend Symmes reported her behavior to church leaders.

During the 1630s, many passenger ships from England, including the *Griffin,* arrived in the Massachusetts Bay Colony.

Aboard the *Griffin*

The *Griffin* made several voyages between England and the Massachusetts Bay Colony. The ship took three months to sail across the Atlantic Ocean. In 1634, Hutchinson and her family made the journey. More than 100 other passengers and 50 crew members were also on board. All of the passengers' belongings and food were packed onto the ship. In addition, a herd of 100 cows shared the cramped space.

Living conditions on the ship were awful. Passengers had to deal with storms, sun, windless days, and sometimes pirates. Food choices were limited. Passengers could eat salted fish, pork, or beef. They also ate hardtack, a dry biscuit.

Life in the Colonies

Boston was a small town in the Massachusetts Bay Colony. In 1630, John Winthrop established the town for Puritans only. Early settlers of the Massachusetts Bay Colony believed that God wanted them to create a "pure" colony. The Puritans believed they were God's chosen people. Winthrop became the first governor of the Massachusetts Bay Colony.

Anne Hutchinson in the Colonies

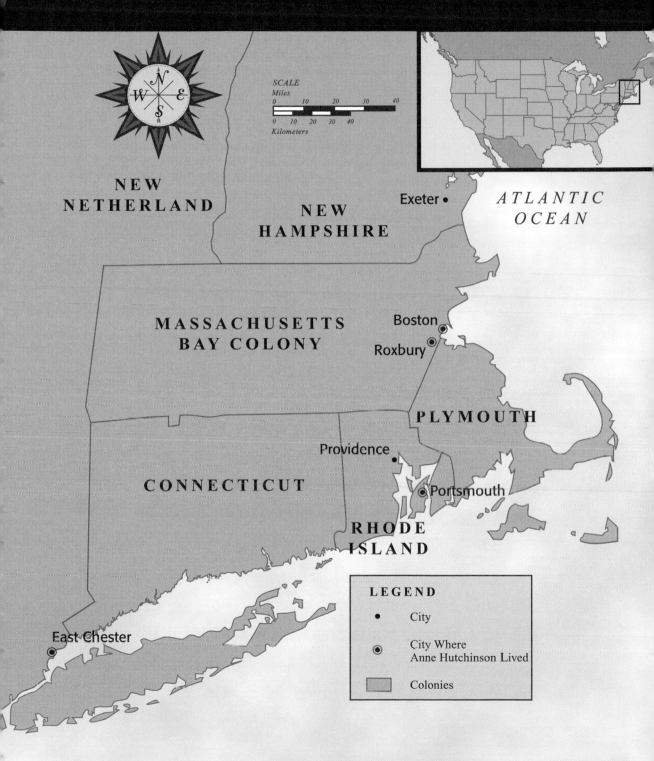

SCALE
Miles
0   10   20   30   40
0   10   30   40
Kilometers

NEW
NETHERLAND

NEW
HAMPSHIRE

Exeter •

ATLANTIC
OCEAN

MASSACHUSETTS
BAY COLONY

Boston ◉
Roxbury ◉

PLYMOUTH

Providence •

CONNECTICUT

◉ Portsmouth

RHODE
ISLAND

East Chester ◉

LEGEND

• City

◉ City Where
   Anne Hutchinson Lived

▭ Colonies

Food in the New World

American Indians introduced many foods to European settlers, including corn. This hearty grain quickly became the main ingredient in many dishes. The settlers used it to make cornmeal bread and succotash, a dish with corn and beans. The American Indians also introduced pumpkin, squash, and turkey to the new settlers. Maple syrup became a popular sweetener.

Hutchinson's friend and teacher John Cotton was a leader of a church in Boston. Unfortunately, the church did not allow new members if one of the leaders objected. Reverend Symmes had objected to Hutchinson's application. Church leaders questioned her beliefs during a special meeting. Hutchinson convinced the leaders that she believed in the Puritan faith. Finally, she was invited to join the church.

Although Hutchinson knew some people from England, almost everything else in Boston was different. Boston winters were much colder than in Alford. Summers were much hotter. The city also had a wide variety of strange new foods.

During the 1600s, it was hard to keep a household running. William stayed busy with his business selling cloth. Hutchinson took care of the children. She and the children had many daily chores. They planted the garden, churned butter, fed the chickens, and collected eggs. Extra food was prepared on Saturdays. The family kept this food for the next day. All work was **forbidden** on Sunday because it was a day of worship.

Puritans in the Massachusetts Bay Colony gathered for church on Sundays. They were forbidden to work on this day of worship.

Government and Church

The government made and enforced religious laws in the Massachusetts Bay Colony. There was no separation between the church and the government. Town meetings and church services were even held in the same meetinghouse.

Laws controlled every part of Puritan life. Puritans were required to attend church on Sundays. Men sat on one side of the meetinghouse and women on the other. Services were held twice a day. All work and play were forbidden on Sunday.

The Puritans wore simple and plain clothing to church and other events. Fancy decorations were not common among most settlers in the Massachusetts Bay Colony.

Hutchinson's Meetings

After joining the church, Hutchinson became popular in Boston. She delivered many babies and helped the sick. She also welcomed women into her home for meetings. During the meetings, Hutchinson explained the previous week's church sermon. She answered questions and expressed her opinions. Hutchinson and the other women also shared healing remedies and tips about children.

Hutchinson became an important person in the Massachusetts Bay Colony. Even women from outside the Boston area began attending the meetings. Sometimes, more than 80 people crowded into her home. Soon, men started attending the meetings. There were so many people at the Thursday gatherings that Hutchinson had to schedule another meeting on Mondays. Her followers became known as Hutchinsonians.

Although she would try to have another baby at age 46, Hutchinson gave birth to her last child in March 1636. She continued holding meetings. Hutchinson was 44 years old.

Chapter Five

Accused

Hutchinson's religious views were different from those of many church leaders. She thought that everyone who truly believed could communicate with God. She did not think that simply following the rules made someone a better person. Hutchinson also believed that women could learn and teach.

John Winthrop and other ministers thought her ideas were dangerous. They believed that only trained ministers could interpret God through the Bible. They also believed that everyone should follow the rules of the church.

Hutchinson disagreed with the church on other issues. She did not support a war against the Pequot Indians in 1637. Hutchinson and her followers refused to send money or men to fight. They also protested against giving large amounts of land to wealthy settlers.

In this painting by Howard Pyle (1853–1911), Hutchinson preaches to some of her followers, who were called Hutchinsonians.

The Pequot War of 1637

During the 1630s, many Puritan settlers arrived in the Massachusetts Bay Colony. As the colony grew, conflicts between settlers and American Indians in the area increased. These conflicts led to the start of the Pequot War in 1637.

Although Hutchinson and her followers refused to support this war, many of the colonists continued to fight. In May 1637, they burned 700 Pequot Indians alive in nearby Connecticut. This battle ended the war with the Pequot but did not end conflicts between settlers and American Indians.

Against the Law

Hutchinson complained about most of the ministers in Boston. She only supported Cotton and her brother-in-law John Wheelwright. Soon, church officials became angry.

In 1637, they called a meeting of ministers from around the colony. The ministers defined acts of **heresy** or ideas that went against the church's teachings. The members of the meeting made a list of 82 items that were not **tolerated**.

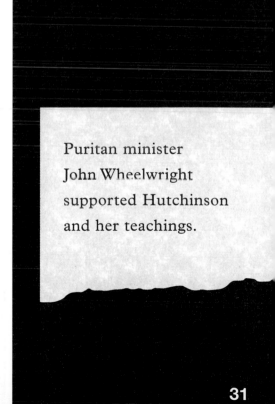

Puritan minister John Wheelwright supported Hutchinson and her teachings.

This document could be used against anyone who did not agree with the church's beliefs. One item the church did not approve of was women holding religious meetings.

Cotton and Wheelwright were part of the meeting. Only Wheelwright refused to vote for the list. He was found guilty of heresy. Wheelwright was also convicted of **sedition**, or rebelling against the government.

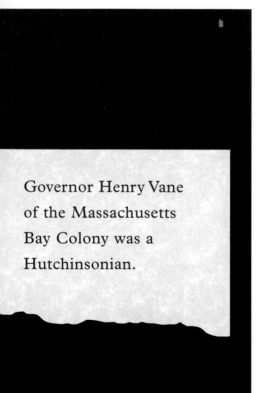

Governor Henry Vane of the Massachusetts Bay Colony was a Hutchinsonian.

During this time, Henry Vane was governor of the Massachusetts Bay Colony. He was also a Hutchinsonian. Vane and other Hutchinsonians wrote a letter asking the court not to punish Wheelwright. Unfortunately, elections came before the court could make a decision. John Winthrop defeated Henry Vane for the position of governor. When Winthrop became governor again, Wheelwright was banished from the colony.

Hutchinson's Trial

In November 1637, Hutchinson went to trial for holding religious meetings. She defended herself in front of the General Court. Governor Winthrop, Reverend Symmes, and John Cotton were all members of the court.

Winthrop accused Hutchinson of holding meetings and breaking a commandment of the Bible. The commandment says to "honor thy father and thy mother." The court members considered themselves Hutchinson's elders. They expected her to treat them with respect.

Hutchinson defended herself without a lawyer. She would not admit to doing anything wrong.

Hutchinson even revealed that God had warned her about the trial. She said God would curse the court for punishing her.

This surprised and angered the court. They believed Hutchinson was lying about her visions from God. Winthrop and the other court members found Hutchinson guilty of heresy and sedition. They sentenced her to banishment.

During her second trial in March 1638, Hutchinson refused to admit that her beliefs were wrong or apologize to the court members.

Banishment

Banishment was a form of punishment that forced a person to leave a town or country. In England, people were banished for not following the Church of England's rules. The Puritans of the Massachusetts Bay Colony also banished many people. Some of these people went on to establish towns in other colonies. After being banished, Reverend John Wheelwright established the town of Exeter, in the area of New Hampshire.

A Second Trial

Hutchinson did not leave Boston immediately. She was placed under house arrest and sent to live in Roxbury, Massachusetts. Hutchinson stayed there for four months. Only her family and ministers were allowed to visit.

In March 1638, the ministers put Hutchinson on trial again. This time, they expected her to admit that her beliefs were wrong and apologize. She refused.

The ministers were furious. They believed she had acted out of place. Reverend John Wilson described Hutchinson as a worker of the devil. Even John Cotton turned against her. Hutchinson was thrown out of the church.

Chapter Six

Later Years

The Hutchinsons had to start over. William had already gone to the area of Rhode Island. He set up a home for his wife and their children. Compared to Massachusetts, Rhode Island was wild and rough. Hutchinson was expecting her 16th child. It was a long journey for her and the children.

The previous months had taken their toll on Hutchinson. After settling into their new home, she had a painful miscarriage. Her unborn baby died. Hutchinson could not get out of bed for months. Her family worried that she too would die. Some ministers believed this was God's punishment.

Hutchinson eventually recovered. She helped establish the town of Portsmouth, Rhode Island, and started preaching to others in her new community.

During the later years of her life, Hutchinson continued to be a strong religious leader to members of her community.

Roger Williams and Rhode Island

In 1631, a young minister named Roger Williams came to Boston. Williams believed that government and religion should be separate. He also believed everyone should be able to choose his or her own religion. In 1636, he was banished from the Massachusetts Bay Colony. Williams went south to the area known as Aquidneck. He bought land from the American Indians and established the town of Providence, Rhode Island. Williams welcomed other brave thinkers, such as the Hutchinsonians.

Although she had moved beyond the power of the church, Winthrop and other officials still feared Hutchinson's influence. They tried to silence her with letters and visits from other ministers. They even put her son and son-in-law in prison. Hutchinson would not stop preaching her beliefs.

Leaving English Territory

In 1642, Hutchinson's husband died. He had been a loving companion and partner. Without William by her side, Hutchinson wanted to move far away.

She took her six youngest children to the Dutch colony of New Netherland, which is now New York. Hutchinson settled in the area of East Chester. Soon, she began preaching again.

Many people warned Hutchinson about the American Indians in the area. She refused to protect her home with guns or other weapons. Hutchinson had lived peacefully with the American Indians in the area of Rhode Island. She believed in living peacefully with all people.

Unfortunately, Hutchinson was not prepared for an attack. In the fall of 1643, a group of American Indians killed Hutchinson and part of her family. Only her youngest daughter survived. Hutchinson was 52 years old.

Throughout her life, Hutchinson defended her religious and political beliefs. She sacrificed her own freedom to fight laws she considered unfair. She stood up for the rights of women and inspired many others to follow. Without courage like Anne Hutchinson's, America's freedom of expression would not be possible.

In 1643, Hutchinson and five of her children were killed by a group of American Indians in the area of East Chester, New York.

A statue in front of the State House in Boston honors Anne Hutchinson and her struggle for religious tolerance.

TIME LINE

Marries William Hutchinson
and moves back to Alford

Born in Alford, England

Sails with husband
and family to the
Massachusetts
Bay Colony

Moves with family
to London

The plague spreads
through Alford; two of
Hutchinson's daughters die.

| 1591 | 1605 | 1607 | 1612 | 1620 | 1630 | 1633 | 1634 |

Pilgrims arrive aboard the
Mayflower and found
the Plymouth Colony.

Settlers from England establish Jamestown
Colony, the first permanent white settlement
in North America.

John Cotton sails to the
Massachusetts Bay Colony
to escape imprisonment
in England.

Sentenced to banishment by John Winthrop and other General Court members of the Massachusetts Bay Colony

William dies; Hutchinson moves to New Netherland with six of her children.

Helps establish the town of Portsmouth, Rhode Island

Killed in an attack by a group of American Indians

| 1636 | 1637 | 1638 | 1642 | 1643 |

Colonists massacre almost 700 Pequot Indians near West Mystic, Connecticut.

Representatives of the colonies of Massachusetts, Connecticut, Plymouth, and New Haven form the United Colonies of New England.

Roger Williams founds Providence, Rhode Island, after being banished from the Massachusetts Bay Colony.

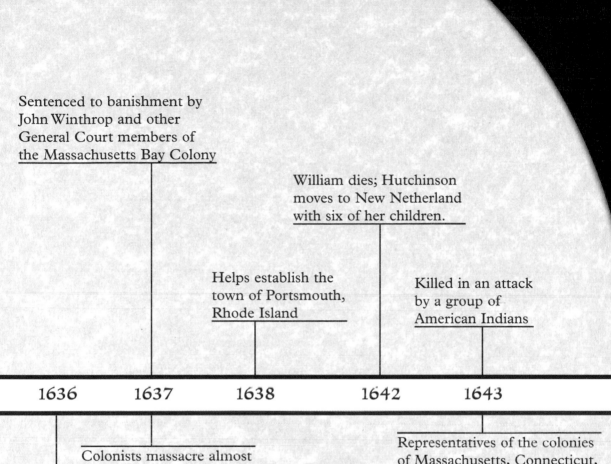

Glossary

banish (BAN-ish)—to send someone away from a place and order the person not to return

communion (kuh-MYOO-nyuhn)—Christian practice in which people eat bread and drink wine or grape juice to remember Jesus Christ

forbidden (fur-BID-in)—not permitted or allowed to do something; Puritans were forbidden from working on Sundays.

heresy (HER-uh-see)—actions or opinions that are different from those of a particular religion or unacceptable to people of authority

plague (PLAYG)—a very serious disease that spreads quickly to many people and often causes death

Puritan (PYOOR-uh-tuhn)—a group of religious people in England during the 1500s and 1600s who wanted simple church services and enforced a strict moral code; many Puritans fled England and settled in America.

remedy (REM-uh-dee)—something that relieves pain, cures a disease, or corrects a disorder

revelation (rev-uh-LAY-shuhn)—something that is revealed by God to humans

sedition (suh-DI-shun)—rebelling or speaking out against lawful authority, such as the church or the government

tolerate (TOL-uh-rate)—to put up with something or endure it; the church would not tolerate Anne Hutchinson's meetings.

Read More

Clark, Beth. *Anne Hutchinson: Religious Leader.* Colonial Leaders. Philadelphia: Chelsea House, 2000.

Colman, Penny. *Girls: A History of Growing Up Female in America.* New York: Scholastic Reference, 2000.

Pell, Ed. *John Winthrop: Governor of the Massachusetts Bay Colony.* Let Freedom Ring. Mankato, Minn.: Capstone Press, 2004.

Peters, Stephanie True. *The Black Death.* Epidemic! New York: Benchmark Books, 2003.

Slavicek, Louise Chipley. *Life Among the Puritans.* The Way People Live. San Diego: Lucent Books, 2001.

Useful Addresses

Bostonian Society
Old State House
206 Washington Street
Boston, MA 02109-1713
The Bostonian Society is
Boston's historical society and
museum. The organization
collects and preserves the history
of Boston.

Founder's Brook Park
Boyd's Lane
Portsmouth, RI 02871
Anne Hutchinson and other
settlers landed in this area of
Rhode Island in 1638.

Massachusetts Statehouse
Beacon and Park Streets
Boston, MA 02116
The center of state government in
Massachusetts features a statue of
religious leader Anne
Hutchinson.

Plimoth Plantation
P.O. Box 1620
Plymouth, MA 02362
A living history museum of
Plymouth, Massachusetts, in
the 1600s. Actors re-create life
during this time period.

Internet Sites

FactHound offers a safe, fun way to find Internet sites related to this book. All of the sites on FactHound have been researched by our staff.

Here's how:
1. Visit *www.facthound.com*
2. Type in this special code **0736824545** for age-appropriate sites. Or enter a search word related to this book for a more general search.

3. Click on the Fetch It button.

FactHound will fetch the best sites for you!

Index